From The Women's Press Ltd
34 Great Sutton Street, London EC1V 0DX

Raving Beauties are a three woman team of actress-singers: Anna Carteret, Sue Jones-Davies and Frances Viner.

Anna Carteret has spent most of her life working in the theatre, particularly at the National Theatre, and has recently attempted roles as diverse as the title role in *Major Barbara* and 'Nora' in *A Doll's House*. Perhaps best known for her role as the police inspector in the BBC television series, *Juliet Bravo*, her recent television credits include *Heat of the Day* and *The Shell Seekers*.

Sue Jones-Davies lives in Wales with her three sons. She is currently working with Raving Beauties and on voice production.

Frances Viner has worked with the Royal Shakespeare Company and the National Theatre. She now acts, directs and writes for Raving Beauties.

In their performances of *In the Pink*, *Make it Work* and *Tea at the Ritz*, Raving Beauties have created catalytic entertainment out of their experiences of growing up, relating, mothering, working and loving. In a new production of *Macbeth* they examine the repression of the feminine.

The group would like to acknowledge other company members who contribute to their evolving performance work: Eluned Jones, Dee Orr and Patricia Franklin; the poet and director Josie Hollis; and their administrator Kate Brooks.

This book is dedicated
to every woman
who sent us a poem.

RAVING BEAUTIES

NO HOLDS BARRED

 The Women's Press

First published by The Women's Press Limited 1985
A member of the Namara Group
34 Great Sutton Street, London EC1V 0DX
Reprinted 1985, 1989

British Library Cataloguing in Publication Data

No holds barred.
  1. English poetry – 20th century
  821'.914'08   PR1225

  ISBN 0-7043-3963-3

Typeset by MC Typeset Limited, Gillingham, Kent
Printed and bound by Cox and Wyman Ltd, Reading, Berks

The following poems have been published in:
Writing Women – 'Soup' by Selima Hill, part of a series of poems
which won a prize at Sotheby's/Arvon poetry competition; *And,
1960* – 'Lament' by Gerda Mayer; *Encounter*, February 1983 – 'Blinis'
by Felicity Napier; *Jestem Baba*, published in Polish by Wydawnictwo
Literackie, Kraków, 1973 – 'The Washerwoman', 'Peasant Woman',
'Mother-to-be in the Milk Bar', 'She Doesn't Want To', 'Her
Greatest Love', 'She Realised', 'No Holds Barred', 'In the Railway
Station', 'The Cow Loves Her', 'Her Belly', 'Two Old Women',
'Immortal' by Anna Świrszczyńska, English translation © Margaret
Marshment and Grazyna Baran, 1985; *Spare Rib* – 'The Heroines'
and
'Latch-Key Kid' by Penny Windsor; *Battle Cries*, published by Astra,
1981 – 'Access' by Astra.

Contents

Foreword

> Consider the inarticulate
> whose unresolved thoughts
> remain unspoken and unwritten.
>
> *Hilda Cohen*

We are proud to have compiled this extraordinary collection of women's poetry.

Ever since our first show, 'In The Pink', based on women's poetry and songs, was shown on Channel Four, we have received a steady trickle of unsolicited poetry from women. This encouraged us to advertise for more to see if we could find enough for a book of unpublished women's poetry.

The response was overwhelming: from established poets, who sent us new work; from unpublished writers striving to get into print; from poets who had never considered publication; and from women who had never written before but did so in response to our appeal. We have included poems from each group.

Whereas our first poetry collection, *In The Pink*, based on our show, included the work of women poets from all over the world, it was our intention in this anthology to concentrate on British poets. We have, however, made one exception. We include translations by Margaret Marshment and Grazyna Baran from the work of the fine Polish poet Anna 'Swir', who died in 1984. We are delighted to publish these poems in English for the first time.

Our advertisement specified an interest in work, ageing, children, violence against women, rape, incest and the nuclear threat – subjects we felt to have been inadequately covered in our first book, because we had not found suitable material. Traditionally, these subjects may not have poetic credibility, but they struck a chord in the thousands of women who wrote to us. These women are challenging male-defined literary criteria, and creating categories for the future.

Our intention was not to limit the range of material, but by suggesting those themes we unleashed a torrent of emotion. The evidence of suffering was devastating and as we read, we found ourselves alternately shocked, depressed and numbed. We are indebted to the courage and vulnerability of those who revealed themselves to us by exposing so many private and painful experiences.

The depth of these experiences was never in doubt, even when the writer failed to grapple effectively with them through language. In trying to achieve a 'poetic' style, many poets lost individuality and impact. We selected those poems which had a gut-eloquence that retained the raw particularity of the event itself. So, to the many women who wrote to us asking for comments on their work, and to whom it was impossible for us to reply individually, we would like to offer this one suggestion: 'Beware of diluting your style!'

Just as there were many poems that persistently made us cry, there were as many others that always made us laugh. It was the lack of compromise common to both which inspired our final selection.

One of the women who wrote to us said that she 'couldn't bear to send her work into a deafening silence'. In this sentence she spoke for many other contributors. They too were haunted by the spectre of '*not good enough!*', this fear of not being listened to.

Yet we women *need* a belief in our ability to communicate, to free ourselves from isolation and give us a voice in the community. Participating in the power that emanates from the shared experience will in turn validate the personal and private self. In editing this book, we want to encourage women in the belief that they are being heard in the public arena.

There *is* someone out there – millions of us!

This book is a distillation of the many, many poems we received, and we would like to think that all the women who wrote to us feel represented in some way. We are privileged to have been the intermediaries between them and all those women and men who read this book.

Anna
Sue
Frances

The Heroines

We are the terraced women
piled row upon row on the sagging, slipping hillsides of our
    lives.
We tug reluctant children up slanting streets
the pushchair wheels wedging in the ruts.
Breathless and bad-tempered we shift the Tesco carrier-bags
    from hand to hand
and stop to watch the town.

The hilltops creep away like children playing games.

Our other children shriek against the schoolyard rails –
    'There's Mandy's mum, John's mum, Dave's mum, Kate's
    mum, Ceri's mother, Tracey's mummy.'
We wave with hands scarred by groceries and too much
    washing-up
catching echoes as we pass of old wild games.

After lunch, more bread and butter, tea,
we dress in blue and white and pink and white checked
    overalls
and do the house and scrub the porch and sweep the street
and clean all the little terraces
up and down and up and down and up and down the hill.

Later, before the end–of–school bell rings,
all the babies are asleep
Mandy's mum joins Ceri's mum across the street
running to avoid the rain
and Dave's mum and John's mum – the others too – stop by
    for tea
and briefly we are wild women
girls with secrets, travellers, engineers, courtesans, and
    stars of fiction, films
plotting our escape like jail–birds
terraced, Tescoed prisoners rising from the household dust
like heroines.

Penny Windsor

I

The Washerwoman

She washes her old man's dirty clothes,
her sons' dirty clothes,
her daughters' dirty clothes.

Inhumanly clean
like her murdered life,
she wipes away at times the sinful tear of a dream
with her clean
washerwoman's hands.

Anna 'Swir'

Hertz So Good

I ride around naked in cars
most of the day
and, when the night comes
I dress and go out to work.

It is good to feel the upholstery
against my skin
sometimes, I just pull in and park
because it's so cool there in the back.

I ride around naked in cars
most of the time
but lately, the boulevards tend
to bother me and the traffic cops
stare at my breasts through the windows.

I shall have to give it up
one of these days
when the hire-charges or the
indecency fines get too much or
else I lose my job.

I tried a strapless swimsuit once
but there was not the
same freedom of movement, and
the plastic bones worked their way
up to the top like wiggly fish.

I ride around naked in cars
most of the day
and, when the night comes
I put on an astrakhan coat and beaver
hat, and hand out advice
at a Marriage Guidance Centre.

Marisa Mitchell

Rape: Married Style

I lie, a bag of flesh
A sack of molecules.
This is not me.
My body is something separate,
Distinct, it surrounds me,
A rubber glove.
Feeling is voluntary.
Rubber glove protect me please.
Let me not feel.
There is a space
Between my legs.
He wants my space.
Laughable really, a hole in a bag.
But my hole, not his.
Not anymore. I married him.
My hole/his hole. Mine, but his.
It's no good
Saying, shouting, pleading, whispering,
'NOOOOOOOO . . .'
It makes no difference.
I used to fight,
But not now, What's the use?
He feeds me and the kids.
Bad day at work?
My space/his aspirin.
I turned my back this time.
Maybe he'd fall asleep.
But I should be so lucky.
No problem. He prides himself. Any angle.
My space, but he's into it all ways.
Should be thankful, he says.
It's not the other spaces.
But sometimes it's them too.
What happens if you bite it?
Could they stitch it up?
Or back on?

4

Probably have you for assault.
'If it please m'lud, I was carried away
Such a delightful taste . . .
Thought it was a juicy carrot.'
Or even better . . .
'If it please m'lud, it was my false teeth.
The kids magnetised the gold.'
Wouldn't do. They'd get you.
'We find you guilty of denying
Your lawful husband his lawful rights
FOR E–e–VER.'
'We sentence you to eat carrots
FOR E–e–VER.'
Someone out there please help me.
Inside this rubber glove the me is shrinking.
Now it's only between the eyes. The rest is other.
He's heaving inside the other,
Finished,
I breathe again.
The me is still there, apart.
He didn't get me. I didn't feel.
And aspirin duty is over again . . .
For today.

Jill Hills

At Last They Have Caught The Ripper

Tonight
in the city of red lights

the man in the street
is nobody's suspect.

They have pinned down
the one villain

whose eyes
were scissors.

The woman
who walks alone

belongs to everyman
again.

His rights
have stitched up the exits.

Gillian Allnutt

The Chidren Sleep
Soundly Upstairs

He enters
the kitchen.
Purposely he
brushes against me.

I'm infested
with rage.

I want to
paralyse him
with a sharp
pair of scissors,

cut him up
like a
feather
pillow

and watch
the stuffing
float into
oblivion.

Broken glass
is spinning
inside
my head.

The children
sleep
soundly
upstairs.

Holly Beeson

Nice Men

I know a nice man who is kind to his wife and always lets her do what she wants.

I heard of another nice man who killed his girlfriend. It was an accident. He pushed her in a quarrel and she split open her skull on the dining-room table. He was such a guilt-ridden sight in court that the jury felt sorry for him.

My friend Aiden is nice. He thinks women are really equal.

There are lots of nice men who help their wives with the shopping and the housework.

And many men, when you are alone with them, say, 'I prefer women. They are so understanding.' This is another example of men being nice.

Some men, when you make a mistake at work, just laugh. They don't go on about it or shout. That's nice.

At times, the most surprising men will say at parties, 'There's a lot to this Women's Lib.' Here again, is a case of men behaving in a nice way.

Another nice thing is that some men are sympathetic when their wives feel unhappy.
I've often heard men say, 'Don't worry about everything so much, dear.'

You hear stories of men who are far more than nice – putting women in lifeboats first, etc.

Sometimes when a man has not been nice, he apologises and trusts you with intimate details of the pressures in his life. This just shows how nice he is, underneath.

I think that is all I can say on the subject of nice men. Thank you.

Dorothy Byrne

But What of the Tigers?

I remember always, his eyes,
a shock, beneath the overhang of brows;
grey–green opaque barriers – not of our kind,
caught at the outside of the lower shape
as if with a stitch . . .

He was bearded then and no one
called him handsome except me.

I, who had an empty place,
took him to fill it – uncaring
of all the danger signs.
Something in him – some blind anguished thing,
unacknowledged and unclaimed,
called to me and I answered . . .
. . . or so it seemed.

His body knew me – sank
thankfully into my soft depths.

I remember his thighs
weakened by polio – the
thick rope of his penis
that gave me my children . . .
. . . and how, when words had ravaged,
my face tight with unfreed tears,
should he batter me again,
in sleep, his hand would find me
and I marvelled at the hate and need.

Slowly, with many backward looks
I took myself from him –
broke the dance of death,
dragged myself, menopause and all
to a place of safety . . .
. . . or so I thought.

9

He too, after posturing aimlessly awhile,
confused without his adversary.

And, having given up on him –
smelling only the stale sweat on his jumper
with no excitement leaping,
then it is, with disbelief at first,
I see his metamorphosis –
taking, at last, responsibility
in some measure –
still in old clothes, spending on the children –
giving me rest – jumble sale finds –
shipping them here in his old banger . . .
mother-eyes, I watch his listing walk.

In the spare room the divan sings
as he, heaving, turns: there is no mattress.

(My heart still flips in terror
at the sound of key in lock
and I put a chair across my door.)

I lie softly in my ochre womb
breathing the jasmine joss-stick
and guarding my sexuality
till my faceless lover comes . . .

but what of the Tigers?

Marie Courtez

access

two days before christmas
the judge orders access
to the two year old
for daddy:
he's been on good behaviour
for the past six months
(while contesting custody)
so the court needn't care about
the belt round
the mother's neck
the hose–pipe down
the step–son's throat
the garden fork
thrown into the children's room
in the early hours
of another christmas

two days before christmas
the judge orders access
for the devoted daddy
(didn't the nursery matron say
the child needed her father?)
he once ran off with the two kids
from his other marriage
which is why this mother
(hiding from him at a refuge)
knows he mustn't be alone
with her daughter

but the judge says
hand over the child
at the local police station
every second sunday
and collect her there
at half past four the same afternoon

the little girl hasn't been consulted
and screams when daddy
drives her off
for a triumphant outing
while the cops pursue their paperwork

at the appointed hour
the child is back
but it's been the longest day
in her mother's life

there is now a fortnight
to prepare for the next instalment:
perhaps devoted daddy will lose interest
and perhaps he won't –
revenge on the wife who ran from him
keeps him going
and going
and going

Astra

Apple Time

He is going to bed in the square red building.
Around him are fields and four more hospitals.
He undresses, draws the curtains round his cot
and takes the pills they have given him.
'Yes,' they say, 'your doctor will come next week.'

In their house, alight with books and pictures,
a red setter, a bird, fish and the new hamster,
the children have taken themselves to bed.
She sits on in the kitchen amongst the litter
of his departure. The receiver is off the hook.

At breakfast he chooses sausages, as before,
signs himselfs up for an hour of creative therapy
and isolates his 5p pieces for the phone.
'Bring the typewriter, I'll have another go –
and I need a padlock for my cupboard door.'

Chin on hands, she is a triangle of hopelessness;
two China tea-leaves cross like swords in her cup.
It's happened again. She sees him spotlit in the hall
last night. She kisses his cheek goodbye,
his knuckles grip white on their weekend case.

By four o'clock he is in the visitors' room,
facing children's television. She should be here.
His mind is thick and light like foam. He doesn't care.
She arrives with chocolate cake and books, the kids,
typewriter and padlock. He cannot speak to her.

'Look at all the apples, children. Nurse said
you could go and pick some to take home with us.'
Turning from the screen they file out silently.
The parents watch them cartwheel on the empty lawn.
'I could make an apple pie for you.' He does not smile.

After them the door is slammed. She hears the easy
click of a lock, the rattle of keys on a belt.
At the window his hand is raised like the Buddha's,
calling the earth to witness. The children bicker
in the car; in front of her is distance and a grey road.

Felicity Napier

Peasant Woman

She carries on her shoulders
the house, the garden, the farm,
the cows, the pigs, the calves and the children.

Her back wonders
why it doesn't break.
Her hands wonder
why they don't fall off.
She doesn't wonder.

Like a bloodstained stick
her dead mother's drudgery
supports her.
They used the lash
on her great-grandmother.

That lash
shines on her through the clouds
instead of the sun.

Anna 'Swir'

Driving Home, Sunday Afternoon

The scream came from my mouth
and splintered the small space
of the car
and inside
my son, and me
in the thick of it

and the scream came again
with almost no break
from one to the next
the car shimmered
in the sound of it

it crashed against the doors
and rose up
behind the windows
it covered our heads
and we sat
me driving
and he
saying nothing

The scream continued
again and
again
my mouth stretched
with its pulling
growing larger and larger
expanding with the sound of it
pounding like fists
and then
it exploded

I threw back my head
and tore open
a passage

and it came
frayed and ready
and crystal clear

The sound of a child
screaming NO
the sound of a woman
ripping open
her past
I watched the surface
of stagnant pain
ripple

My hair
stood
around my head
as I drove
my son sitting behind me
and me
screaming.

Back-Tracking

Here is where I started from,
Crawling from this big corrupt bloom,
Trailing passion in the sunburnt alleys,
Teenaged and turning from my roots.
Now I bring my kids here –
They snivel and whine at my heels,
A pack of scuffling dogs,
They cannot scent the passion in the streets.
　　I've rather lost the knack myself.

I see myself in the gorgeous striding girls
But reflected in plate glass
A drab little Jenny Wren stares back aghast,
Body as lumpen as the shopping bag.
Marriage is made in heaven, he said.
I think it's made by Sony in Japan.
Nightly we monitor the TV screen,
He smokes, I sit and think:
　　Heaven stubbed out in little pieces.

Later the crude mechanics in the dark,
The panting-by-numbers job,
Me and my Pavlovian responses,
Once a brushing kiss would bring me gasping to my knees.
Now I find myself compiling lists
Or remembering a park bench in spring rain,
Quick and fifteen, I was, leaning towards summer.
Ambition in my eyes, some vivid hopes
　　And all the future burning in my palm.

Judy Lovett

Friday Nights

Noreen goes there every Friday with Brenda.
She hopes Barry will send her a message over from the other
    side
(and eventually be his bride),
She is wearing her best pink dress
and her green patent leather shoes.
She looks a mess.
So does Brenda.
Big friend of hers.
Boys laugh as she passes,
laugh as the strobe bounces off her glasses.
Brenda's bottom has been pinched by Barry's mate.
Is this some sort of sign?
Will Barry aquiesce?
She can only guess.
God, the torture of these Friday Nights, this hateful place.
Still she must endure it, she must.
In the power of love she must place her trust.

Philomena Broderick

I Don't Want To, I Don't Want To Do This

I don't want to, I don't want to do this.

Pick me up and put me where you want me, it's not impossible. Down in your socks, deep in your wallet, hang me small from your ear and I'll whisper to you. But I still don't want to do this, it's not as easy as you think.

Let me tell you what I've been doing today, I want to tell you because it's what I am, it's the most important thing about me, and I don't think you know, I don't think you know what it is you're fucking.

My daily functions are important, it's how I spend my time, it's the snapshot truth of my life and there's not much time left over. Is that the little piece that you want? Is that the little polyunsaturated piece that you like fucking?
That little piece is like an old diary – it's years out of date.

Today and yesterday and last month and last year I got out of bed and started to work. I fed and washed and dressed myself and then I did the same again to someone else. I cleaned and wiped, scraped, coaxed and soaked. I pushed, unpacked, pressed and wrote the lists I write to keep the whole thing from slipping from me.

Sometimes I forget what I have to do next. At this time I cream my hands, I do this three or four times in a day.

At some point I leave the house, but not before I've closed the windows, checked the locks and switches and put on my coat and gloves and then I put coat, gloves and a hat on someone else.

I pay out little piles of money that I collect each week to keep things ticking over. I have tiny bombs in my head and I have to do certain things to stop them exploding. Once I've paid out I can start to gather things in again and then I begin to separate. I always try to rearrange the separations, it makes the same things seem different.

When I come home it all begins again.
I wash, wipe, untie, take off. Small steps done to make space
for the next step and so on and so on. It's a necessary process.

When I've finished my daily functions I make a list for the
next day and then I cream my hands. At this time of the day
they are rough and cracked, creaming them feels good, I
work it in, hard and then soft and they feel quiet again.

What's left over after all this is done is thin and hard to get
hold of, a nylon thread on the carpet. I have to tread carefully
because it's difficult to walk on something so thin and I'm not
a real acrobat.

This line, this poor imitation is what you fuck, it's what you
work on.
I can feel it cracking beneath your fingers.

J. Hollis

Afterwards

He ran the bath and (emptying her bottle of herbal oil) said:
'Take some aspirin, hop right into bed. I'll make some tea.
Poor kid, just look at the state of you.'
Teeth chattering, she lay rigid in the hot, greasy-sweet water.
The tips of her hair floated like weeds.
He came back with the cup sending steam into the steam.
'Here you are then, drink it up.'
But her jagged hand wouldn't work, one of those
dreams where you want to run but get stuck.
The lazy tea-stain sprawled in the bath water,
and she scrambled away from it to the other side.
'Now then, clumsy, no need to waste it. If you
didn't want it, you only had to say . . .'

Beverley Ireland

Choosing My Words Carefully

Choosing my words carefully
   that I may not hear the sound
   of my own voice . . .

He slowly, deliberately sheds his
   family-man clothes,
   leaving them to drop –
   a heap of discarded responsibilities to the floor
Silently and relentlessly forcing
   me downwards,
peeling off my protective layers
   of childhood
   to join his –
a symbolic joining together of
   outward conformities.

'I won't hurt you.
Trust me.'

His tongue, wet and snake-like
   probes hard and insistent
   making it difficult for me to breathe.
Caresses, not clenched fists
   come at me
   covering my body with guilt
   instead of bruises.

               Can others see my secret?
               Smell my uncleanness?

I gaze, transfixed as a frightened
   rabbit in the car
   headlights at his penis
   (should it be nameless as terror?)
   growing, thrusting out
   towards me,
   pushing between my legs.

'Trust me.
I am your father.'

Suddenly, pumping warm stickiness
    over my belly.
I try hard not to vomit.
Afraid of my femaleness
    he does not enter.
Pregnancy means prison
    (for him – what for me?)

Trust me damn you!
                    Is it always to be like this?
                    Is it always pain and fear?

Forcing my inexpert hands
    and mouth to perform
    for his gratification.
I die inside
    for who can touch me now?

                            I am alone with my
                            guilt and self-hate.

I slowly don my armour
    against the world and myself,
    my clothes of innocence
    and creep out of his
    naked presence
    to face a mother awash in drink and hatred.
My secret intact
    in spite of the lingering,
    sickening taste and smell of his maleness.
My concept of love forever destroyed.

Rowena Hall

His Father's Son

The small boy pisses
In the grocer's shop.
The old women's faces break
In flaccid grins.
The small boy enjoys
Watching them more
Than Play School.
Now blushing, they
Tell me he's
His father's son, grab
The counter cloth,
Chase the urine across
The floor,
Down the polished step.
The small boy's shackled,
Pants round ankles,
Stumbles, plants his
Hands on the bent woman's
Fat buttocks. Giggling,
She rewards him with
A Mars Bar,
Turns,
Replaces the cloth on the counter.

Maggie Hannan

Mother-to-be in the Milk Bar

The very young mother-to-be
pours milk into a mug.
After eight hours on her feet
her legs are puffy.

But in her heart there flies about
on little rose-coloured wings
the little bib
she bought the day before.

Anna 'Swir'

Emperor Baby

Your tiny heavy head
Gossed in ginger gold and red
Worked against my marble breast
Doggedly fetching upstream
Till the veins snaked down bluish-green
And I sat up all night holding you
A weary drunken queen.

At one year a Buddha-king
You make the dead objects dance and sing
Bring grace to carpet fluff and string
See diamonds in the dust
Below the lampshade's brim
Your fingers trace
The connections across my face.

All my days are measured in your hours
Clamped by satin gums
I am sucked dry
Undone by your desires
Hooked to me by your green-sea eyes
Your life is a weight
Passing through me
On a thin line to earth.

Jehane Markham

and

and
he cried
and I turned
and spilt my half-snatched tea
and
I wiped up
and the milk boiled over
and he cried
and I'd run out of tissues
and he flung his rusk
down on the littered floor

then days of endless chores
and endless broken nights
took him by the ankles
and swung his head against the wall
and a thousand dirty nappies
dribbled bibs
threw him across the room
and doors without number slammed in my face –
jobs, clubs, classes, pubs, parties, holidays –
lost worlds of freedom –
smashed him in the mouth and jumped on his ribs . . .

and when
I'd slapped him
he cried
and I cried
and no one wiped my tears
either
and he cried
and

Fay Chivers

Brain–Damaged

Nights were always the worst.
He used to cry out
at frequent intervals –
wild, inhuman sounds
compounded of nothing we could comprehend.

And every time I would go to him
in case – just this once –
he might have need of comforting . . .

But, alien at the cot's end,
he would stand and stare
at his own stark world
which I could not enter.

Margot Stewart

Case History

It was her own cry
Cracked each night to starry fragments;
Her own hunger
Greedy for milk, draining her seas dry.
It was her own sorrow
Sobbed all day in the empty rooms without cause;
Her own throat
Where the hands tightened.
Prisoned in blankets
Instinct gropes for the child she overlaid;
Her ignorant breast
Weeps to the pull, pull, of the dumb mouth.

Angela Costen

Being There

My child called my name in the street as I rushed past,
 unseeing.
Later I turned, and saw her stricken face,
The one she'll wear when she is old
When in a dream she'll call my name, and I,
Having joined the dead, rush on –
Not as today, turn back
To clasp her in my arms.

Ethel Portnoy

Love Poem

You are my child
I love you.

I love the roundness of your limbs
Your bottom curves in the palm of my hand.
Where your head ends and your neck begins
Lies a delicious nook
Edged with curls.
Your laughing eyes devour me.
Your legs are podgy, sturdy:
The dimples in your hands
Dissolve me.

And when the tension mounts,
When the hours of playing, feeding, changing,
Watching, waiting
Wear me down . . .
I look at your bonny bottom
And I relent.

You are my child
And I love you.

Ann Hunter

A Sequence of Poems for my Daughter, Christmas '83

I

Why are you in bed, Mama?

I'm tired,
The part of me that kept my back straight
And my hands busy with
    cooking
    cleaning
    caring
has broken.
I'm tired.

Why are you crying Mama?

I'm unhappy.
The part of me that kept my mouth smiling
and my heart busy with
    caring,
    soothing,
    coping,
has broken.
I'm unhappy.

II

Mothers should not cry,
    or lie in bed.
My mother did not lie in bed and cry –
She had five of us, there was no time.
I, who have only one, have time enough.
I am worn out trying to be too many people –
Mother, father,
I try all roles – breadwinner, housekeeper.

My mother had a maid.
If I am too tired, the housework does not get done,

33

We have chips for dinner,
And the dishes pile up like guilt in the sink.

How can I expect you to understand?
You are twelve and
    twelve is a time for being twelve and silly.
How grey my thoughts are today.
I cannot be all that you expect of me
    any more than
You can be all I expect of you.

III

For my Christmas present next year
I would like:
    someone else to be mother
    someone else to buy the presents
    (and worry if we can afford them)
    someone else to buy the food
    and do the cooking –
While I take a long walk in the country
    by myself.

IV

When you were young
You took the love I gave you
And gave me all you had,
Held nothing back.
Things were easier then.

Now, twelve years from the womb
You face me:
    'This is what I am,' you say,
    'This is who I am.
    You gave me life (a dubious gift –
    double-edged, welcome and unwelcome)
Now you have to live with me.'

Well, that is so,

and we are bound as inextricably to each other
as if the birthcord had never been cut,
pulling and pushing.
Why did I think it would be easy?

V

I love you –
Child of my womb
Child of my heart
Pain-bringer
Love-giver
Joy-maker
Time-taker
Heart-healer
Daughter mine.

Debi Hinton

She Doesn't Want To

Her mother
suffered her whole life.
And bore her
to suffer too.

But she doesn't want to suffer.
She hates
her mother.

She stretches her fists to the sky,
and with her fists
she writes across the sky
from horizon to horizon:
– I don't want to.

Anna 'Swir'

Three Years Old
To E.R. (1912 – 1979)

Smiling dad and daughter
for girls
curls
and fashion sailor-suited then
blue skirt;
it was an earlier era

nearer father came
smiling
admiring
manly sailor true
in his sailor blue
she smiled at him too
as any other afternoon.

The bed?
on her back put flat
sailor placed her flat
unclipped his Jack Tar's knife
her skirt pulled up to her neck;
he'd never before done that.
to change?
face; strange . . .

re-dressing . . . silent pain
muted as she'd lain
mumbling to query dad
fumbling in her haze
horror in her gaze.

Across her neck, his knife;
'If you ever tell . . .';
slowly snaked that knife.

Six years old
still mute, none told
in school; at home;

she'd grown.
Paler; passive; ever prone;
never amused; still abused;
still mute; none told;
at six years old
she'd grown.

Mum and dad conferred
daughter to country sent
to talk; to try
to talk; not baulk.
then chat began;
but not: 'the knife!'
not: 'the pain!'
not: 'dad has changed!'
'the knife'; 'the pain!'

Eleven years old;
mum and dad they told
the so-called facts of life;
but not the pain and not the knife.
Eleven years old and told
the so-called facts of life.

At twenty-four years old
told her dad had died;
on the road;
crashed prone;
and dead.

Funeral wake
family there
everywhere
everyone
in the home
where she'd lain prone.
Queries fluffed the room;
'Why a daughter calm?
so cold, so calm, remote,

no grief, no tears, so cold?'
She told.

All stalled
appalled;
mother already in grief
her sailor husband gone;
all stalled
appalled;
her sailor father gone;
she 'told'.
'I'm glad he's dead', she said;
'I'm glad he's dead and gone!'

and I'd only asked
my middle-aged friend
with two years' friendship passed
her first memory in life.

Greta Gordon-Heath

Documentary

After I made myself watch the film
I had a nightmare about driving.
A face in the windscreen sliding towards me
screamed forever . . .
like the Somali child held down by relatives
while her aunt circumcised her.

The two cars twisted and stabbed
our muffled flesh like the husband
who used a kitchen knife to penetrate
his tightly-stitched bride.

Next day I searched for photographs
of my daughter at three;
sitting naked on a wicker stool,
her small cunt plump as a dented peach

and shuddered that any god
could want such softness culled.

Patricia Pogson

Cervix

My fingers reach inside
trying to locate the ugly
vowels and consonants
that give my wet flesh
identity with others
of my kind.
Strange that a man
should have found
this first, scored
like a football straight
inside my gut.
Then I was seventeen.
Five years have brought
my own hand as far as
this. A brisk efficient
book described the place.
I squatted as directed on a chair
opened myself and recognised
it, soft as a baby chin –
without help or resignation
or duress.
Two fingers through the film
of ignorance.

Lindsay Macrae

Changing

Crutch slipping towel over
bobbing white bottoms,
my mother said: 'Turn your back to the cave's mouth.'
Fighting wet one-piece skin
over the thighs,
my mother said: 'Someone's coming.'
Caught on a toe, peeling the leg elastic through,
but bottoms are rude –
hide the flat chest hairless groove?
My mother said 'Take a large towel.'
Back in the damp sucking tide-line cave
knickers on first, sticking,
towel trapped by vest, keep it down, keep it down.
My mother said: 'Something is showing.'
Button up. 'I'm decent,' I said.

Plunge in the pool, hair drifting, breasts drifting.
I'm fifty, I'm naked, I'm decent, I said.

Daphne Rock

Too Old at 55

At half-past six, I surfaced from my dream
and drew my parts together, meeting the May morning
in the brilliant sunshine of the bathroom –
Oh God! – crept downstairs – admired my bargain curtains
lugged from the market yesterday – they're second-hand –
great peacocks striding green and blue . . .

I'm tired – my gallant heart is tired – I've learned
at last to love the poor mistaken creature that I was:
I married twice and scarred my body having babes:
with energy and risk, I gave my years –
spinning out the money – endless washdays –
husband turning from me in our bed: should I complain,
he punished me with hitting or desertion . . .

Now, my children open clear eyes on a Friday –
the kitchen waits beflowered and wholesome,
for their breakfast visit – then I am alone –
take out my single-parent state – examine it again,
weighing the gains – pure limbs – no night-time semen stays –
how strangely young my face – no dinner plan –
no black hairs in the sink . . .

Each Wednesday night I mount my bike, and in white jeans
purr gently past the almonds to the club:
I have no lack of partners, for my dance is soul –
the disco lights are red inside my head – long hair flies –
but when I mention 'grandchild', there is a sudden freeze
with calculations . . . yet . . . I need . . . I need –
but what – what is appropriate today? Why, why this
     stubborn
image of total contact – sliding skins and white-teethed
     laughter
that sends me home alone to warm milk and a new virginity?

Marie Courtez

Lament

Youth my
youth you lie
dead your vi
olent vi
olet passions and
follies your
silly green
hopes crushed
your grey
wind that
roared through
the world
pricked and de
flated
your gold–hoofed
high blood
slug
gish and te
thered
your hys
terical
fountains
dry
whilst I
sit in
my e
nor
mous
ramshackle
ego
tistical house
a fat mid
dle aged wo
man smel
ling of
onions

Gerda Mayer

The Old Worcester Women, 1945

Calling over the carrot field
calling across the years
the old Worcester women in wartime

Is this one big enough for you dear
is this one big enough?

Young Elsie simpers
young Ivy smilesgrim
Myrtle snorts a chortle
I titter *hee-hee*
we are
the young ladies of the carrot field
not joining in
not talking bawdy

Over the frosty field
to warm up the dawn
and is this one
big enough dear is this one
big enough for you?

Only one voice
genteelly
holds out
day after day

This one goes right
down to Austrilyer

Nothing would turn them though
from the subject in hand

Gerda Mayer

My Mother-in-Law Pickled Walnuts

My mother-in-law pickled walnuts
and covered floors in rag rugs
she bottomed the house each spring,
crocheted miles of fine lace;
walked with a stick:
Muriel Rock.

Death revealed another woman
who ran away from respectable Blackburn, exchanged
decorous songs by the piano
for one-week stands with Carl Rosa
(Blackpool, Harrogate, Middlesbrough, Leeds,
Scarborough, Hartlepool, Hull)
Sang 'Aida' at the Theatre Royal
(much praised in the *Sunderland Echo*)
had pals in digs: Clara, Minnie and May.

Sea-going men
kept pictures of her draped in braided silk;
Muriel Sancton.

She married a Norwegian sailor, suddenly
(who died, suddenly):

Then she married Thomas Rock.

Daphne Rock

Lamentoso

I want it to be known why
My grandmother never became
The pianist of fame
She so wanted to be.
For years with this aim she practised –
Mornings, afternoons, evenings;
Scales and arpeggios,
Czerny, scherzinos – everything endlessly . . .
Bach, Auber, Debussy, concertos
Stirring glissandos –
She glistened with brilliance on the keys –
Which never pleased or made her father proud,
Support from him withdrawn,
She took marriage vows.
An aloof, distant woman . . . it stifled her
Smothered her, covered her –
Yet she nourished her husband and babies
All of her days. Never using
Her doctorate talent to play
With an orchestra. Just quietly forgot.
And in the back room would modestly teach
Spotty schoolchildren, scales and glissandos
For half-a-crown each.

When she died we never knew if
Pride or regret made my grandfather
Find her certificates, yellowed with years.
Carefully, he framed and hung all sixteen
Around their humble house walls
Each one marked 'with distinction'.

One day, sad and low, he
Pointed to them and said: 'See!
How brilliant she was before marrying me.'

Jenny Weller

A Day at the Seaside

Walking into the sea at Saltburn.
He drove the car. Not talking.
There was bread for tea. And milk.
Two loaves.
She must have been to the corner shop twice.
It makes him angry.
Shells pinch through her thin shoes.
No . . . she is wearing her slippers.
He takes out the one chair
and sits on it.
She has left the dishes and the dirty table.
An eye of spilt milk
stared back at her.
The sun is hot.
She's lost the dishcloth.
He is asleep.
The woman dreams of other days
When she was five and danced in the sea
and the sand ran like honey through her fingers.
She wraps her child around her
and shuffles to the sea.
An old woman alone.
The man is asleep. His fishing-hat hiding his face.
It keeps the wasps away.
He does the washing now.
She gets lost on the way to the launderette
and has to be brought back home.
The sea is cold.
It was warm then.
She must do the dishes.
No one sees her.
Is it Tuesday?
She smiles and lies down.
The bowl of sky
her best blue china
breaks into fragments.   *Mary Brownescombe Heller*

48

Non Sequitur

He won't accept
That she can't walk again.
His eighty Polish
Years have only known
Survival, at a cost.
Defeat has no space in his alphabet.
His blue eyes stare out
Any death.
He buried loss with life.

But now he hears
And sees her harsh decline.
And not one comma
Of his bullying love
Can force and free
Her paralysing bones.
Aside she whispers:
'Ich bin lebensmud.' 'I am tired of living.'
His ostrich feathers
Tremble in the wind.

Lotte Kramer

Two People

Two people
clutching their loneliness
walk across the shingle
and hate each other.

She is in love and
imbecilic
he is aching
and mad.

This is Worthing
he says
and grinds his teeth.
A private goose-step.

Further and further they go
heading for Brighton.
She stops in front of an hotel
and turns to watch as
a dog climbs on to
the back of another.

Feasting on the jerks
and watery eyes of the
docile bitch
he kisses her
chapped lips.

J. Hollis

Her Greatest Love

At sixty she's experiencing
the greatest love of her life.

She walks arm in arm with her lover,
the wind ruffles their grey hair.

Her lover says:
– 'You have hair like pearls.'

Her children say:
– 'You silly old fool.'

Anna 'Swir'

A Beautiful Woman

My darling, I feel so lonely
in this bed that sticks out
from the wall like Cap Blanc Nez
into the English Channel.

You seem to be taking
as long in your bath
as Captain Webb swimming
to France by moonlight.

With his body greased
in porpoise oil,
and eye-protectors
tied on to his ears,

he dived into the sea
at Dover as the local band
struck up 'The Keel Row'
on the promenade.

Yellow starfish stung him,
stung him on the shoulder
and cold, massed seaweed
clung on to his legs.

It was early morning
when he reached Calais.
A beautiful woman
who had waited for him

all night, with beef tea
and candles and delicious cake,
had gone back home
for a decent sleep.

Selima Hill

Domestos

Baking the pubic hair until crisp and tender
the chicken skin
'Darling shall we begin?' she says.

'But the washing machine is full of potatoes, was it you who
put them in?'

'No dear, I'm frying my knickers in bacon fat,
and my stockings crawl in the oven.
I dream of a meal as neat as a pillow,
Husband, greedy tongue,
lick me.'

She buys him steak, and he puts it inside her,
whirling in vegetable confusion.

She learns to faint and equates
polished surfaces with health.

His clothes are all planted in the garden to grow,
    we
    must
    cream
    off
    your
    perfection.
Her husband spits and eats meat, red meat,
pegged out in the world to dry.

Baking her bras until crisp and tender,
'Eat,' she commands,
'For I know your hunger,
husband greedy tongue,
lick me.'

Each bite may explode in his mouth.

Stella Decorum

53

Things To Do

This is my life; this is where I live now in this horrid little
terrace that falls apart faster than it can be put back
together, / with the permanent sounds of family discord
through either boundary wall. / This is my half-hearted
existence, pacing from room to room looking for a surface
to dust, / a floor to sweep, but never wielding polish or
broom with any sincerity of purpose. / Here is my kitchen
where I find myself staring with martyred passion at the
dirty cups and saucers and plates and dishes of yesterday's
breakfast. Here I tread the soapy furrow of the new bride /
from rumbling tub to Spinarinse that sways in its dervish
whirl located somewhere in the steam. / In here I dream of
packing dirty sheets and towels into the front of a
gratefully wide-mouthed automatic machine, / which
would then mean I had more time to sit and stare / at the
tiny collection of frozen peas that rot between cooker and
fridge.

Fiona Pearce

Pin Money

On Friday mornings
the whole estate smelt of glue.
The women were sticking tassels
on to lampshades,
earning their pin money.

On Friday evenings
queuing for their pay,
the women stood,
legs thin as pins,

while the men waited in the pubs,
thick and powerful as magnets.

Valerie Sinason

Boggerel

I wonder why men piss on the floor?
Is it down to aggravation?
Neglect or lack of concentration?
Are they lost in such abstractions
That they lack mundane reactions?
Is it simply they don't see
In which direction that they pee?
Do they do it to annoy?
Do they practise when a boy?
Don't they know the pong it makes,
Those nasty smelly little lakes?
In the wee small hours with feet all bare
It makes a most disgusting snare.
Could it be that men know well
Regardless of the horrid smell
When it comes to cleaning floors
It's females do the rotten chores
Awareness should be raised on this,
This woman's sick of cleaning piss.

Maureen Foster

Ye Housewyf

Ther was a housewyf, strong and coarse of hände,
Who loved the sink the least in all the lands,
A coverchief hadde she upon hir head
Fetis it were and eek of scarlet reed,
Lank hänge hir lockès, straight and blonde of hewe,
For she usèd peroxide, and this is trewe,
And lo! Somethyne to shock the toun,
Hänged from hir fulle red lippës doun
A cygarette, of brande Woodbyne,
Filtre-tipped, and of tobacco fyne.
   Whenne she hadde prepared her husbande's tea,
Chippës fyne, and fisher fingers three,
Hastily sped she hither to the toun,
For Byngo loved she mo than anythynge.
For all thes faults, wel coude she carp and synge.

Meg Wanless

Slut

The ways of the slut have got me // now I don't wash my
hands until I've / lit the stove / for immediate heat / put on the
kettle / peeled a carrot / to chew for immediate comfort /
washed a potato and cut up an onion / a parsnip / and put
them all in the pot

Nor do I wipe my fingers before I've / filled the two paraffin
heaters / run round the wicks with the cutter to clean them /
pulled down the guard on the big one and lit it / and played
the adjustment to get the flame right

When I have picked up / yesterday's underclothes /
yesterday's socks and / folded the dressing gown / remade the
bed and / relaid the table / taken the beans out the fridge /
and fried them / filled up the pepper mill / unstuck the salt // I
sit on the sweater I keep as a cushion and /

eat with my hands dirty // I like them

Mary Michaels

A Woman's Right to Choose

'I haven't had time.'
Words I cannot utter without guilt.
'If you really want to do something
You can make time.'
Make it, how?
Do I go to the three sisters
Dark and secret
And stay a gnarled, cold hand?
Will the skein stop?
Will the many–webbed
And softly pulling thread
Tremble still at my bidding?
I can wind wool,
Deftly weave it,
Even knit.
But make time?
Moon–child of the Goddess, maybe . . .
But powerful enough to
Change the ordered ticking of the world?
No.

Of course,
I could change my priorities.

Why can't people say what they mean?

Ann Hunter

Scores of People Live in Her

Scores of people live in her
Each different face
Wheeled out as appropriate
To fill each different space.
Aria, hymn, pop or folk,
She sings them all to order.
The wise friend
Succeeds the screaming shrew,
With scarcely a pause
The quiet gardener with trowel and trug
Changes places with the critical consumer comparing lipstick
And testing face-cream,
Becomes the peace demonstrator
In jeans and anorak.
The wiper of noses and drier of tears
Charlston's in the sitting-room, unseen.
The opera lover discriminating carefully
From her velvet seat
On her knees
Wipes mud and spilt food from the kitchen floor.
One man's muse, another's virago,
She juggles conservative friends
With radical neighbours,
Breakfasts with *The Times*
And lunches with 'The Archers'
And types the words of others in between.
Spinning like a Catherine wheel
Flinging sparks in all directions
She is quickly consumed.

Barbara Abbs

She Realised

On Sunday afternoon
with the washing–up finally done,
she sat down
in front of the mirror.

And she realised
on Sunday afternoon
that she'd been robbed of her life.

A long time ago.

Anna 'Swir'

No Holds Barred

I catch hold of different things:
snow, trees, useless telephone calls,
the tenderness of a child, journeys,
Rozewicz's poetry,
sleep, apples, morning exercises,
conversations about the salutary properties of vitamins,
exhibitions of avant–garde art,
walks on Kosciuszko's mound, politics,
Penderecki's music,
natural disasters in foreign countries,
the joy of morality and the joy of immorality,
gossip, a cold shower, fashion magazines from abroad,
learning Italian,
a fondness for dogs, the calendar.

I catch hold of everything,
so as not to fall
into the abyss.

Anna 'Swir'

Standing Still

Standing still, standing my ground, something separates me.
I feel it creeping across my shoulder-blades, seeping
through my socks; it's never far away.
Is it this part of me, this part between my legs? Is this where
the separation begins?
Like a cracked egg I stand and watch it make a small stain on
the floor.

J. Hollis

Elegy for Margaret Hall

Born fatherless, to a rough estate –
blessed with deafness, a cleft palate,
found subnormal – though the jokes
you laughed at knew otherwise –
put to work as a chambermaid
in a private hotel; you became
the owner's pet: a sheltered round
of flicks, whist, dusting.

When she died you were forty
and quite unfit for the fifties.
Social workers took over,
placed you in a hospital kitchen,
but like a truant teenager
you kept sloping off for a fag,
lowered your head when spoken to,
spat at threats of discipline.

You were my husband's client,
kept on when he retired.
Over the years you blossomed:
accepted a hearing aid,
began to stop for a chat as you
toddled round window shopping
– the endearing flusters
you got into over money.

Last years were best, making
soft toys in the Day Centre,
coach trips to Morecambe –
small, plump, trusting – until
cancer caught you by the throat;
grew into your chest, abdomen.
He's out arranging your funeral,
trying to find your mother's second name.

It's time to give away your clothes,
take down the list I pinned to the wall

of things you could still eat.
Your sister is too weak for funerals.
If the undertaker can find
your mother's grave there'll be
no need for a new one.

You will be back where you began.

Patricia Pogson

Grandmother

I watched her die.

Not true.
I merely watched her dying
watched her
shrink each day
retreating into her chair.

Often it was I
who emptied her waste
carrying her out
pouring her away.

K. Lindsay

Please Don't

PLEASE DON'T

I met you in the dark alley of the hall carpet. I said, I'm going home now. But suddenly a stranger, you smiled.

PLEA EVEN SO

Nose down on the carpet, sniffing and dust and cat hairs. Lie still and wait. Years later a theory – perhaps that's where the smiles went. Ground down into the shagpile. Perhaps waiting to be hoovered, to be picked out of the dustbag and licked clean like pearls.

FLEE NOTHING SO

Of course, he couldn't keep it hard. Not when she lay like a rag doll. When she had struggled, then it stuck out from his trousers like:

> a fat fish
> a full wallet
> a clenched fist

But when fear made her weak and she pissed herself, then it shrunk and hung like a turkey neck in a butcher's window, damp and bloodless between angry thighs.

PLEASE NOT THAT

The white face all smiles gone, looks up sick
and reproachful (she doesn't look nice like this, not
blubbering, blubbering with fright and soaked in piss).
He pauses, one hand around her throat. Take a body,
    anybody.
(What do I want with her?) 1st doctor: *Tut.* 2nd doctor:
What, not another one been masturbating with the
kitchen knife? I know what happens next. I have a book.
Perhaps I should get her to . . .?

LEASE TAKEN

(Now it's a question of pride. I tried, I tried, you couldn't say didn't try. I couldn't conjure up desire. For all my rubbing up and down her stiff body and sneaking in her mouth with a thick beery tongue it stays soft. She doesn't taste nice. I think the little fool's been sick. I'll make her move.) His hand cracks across her face. She starts to move but a second blow stills her. If asked he could not have said what made him use the knife. Cut and thrust. This is what they mean by it, she thought as she felt the steel penis. An even later theory is that the smiles drained away with the blood dripping themselves along the hall to the telephone, the bathroom, and finally the hospital ward.

EASE EVERYTHING

The blood they gave her back was cold, unfortunately, fresh from the freezer. Her boyfriend remarked upon its icy quality as she screamed at him to take away his hand. The relationship, she said, was terminated. Take your prick elsewhere.

PEACE NOW TAKEN

And what does happen when the scream sticks in your throat, when your whole life hinges on the swing of that scream, but it sticks like cottonwool gags, like the hot mist of vomit, what is there to do? And isn't it funny how even at these moments you think of other things, of . . .

SEE NOTHING NOW

. . . of falling over in the schoolyard, not the hurt but the looking-up and seeing the big girls laughing out of the tall windows. Not the hurt but being seen – Oh, give me the knife and I'll do it myself, but don't lie here heavy knocking the breath out of my lungs with each awkward bump of your body. Did you know that you smell? Did you know that this is hurting me? Did you know that I am trying to scream?

PLEASE NOT THAT SO

Picking herself up slowly she thought *Is this the way it's going to be*? Take a body, anybody's.

PLEASE LEAVE NOW

I met him in the dark alley of the gloomy hall floor.
As he left I tried to call him back. I said

**PLEASE LEAVE NOTHING NOW THAT YOU HAVE
TAKEN EVERYTHING.**

Emma Bolland

Infidelity

The deed was done tactfully.
Black hairs brushed from the bed,
Lips lingering on mine, bathed away.
I'm squeaky clean,
Ready for anything,
Although the smell of sex still lies
Sweetly darkly sleeping on the pillows.

For infidelity is just a state of mind.
The mind recalls your arm
Thrown over me protectively in sleep.
Moments of love after passion,
Just moments.
And I wonder who the hell he is
And where you are.

Jill Penny

Concrete & Clay

We lay there a long time, really,
Chilling to the draught which blew beneath the door.
We were like statues, weren't we,
One above the other like folded rocks,
Massive in our contentment.
It mattered to us then,
If you remember,
Fleetingly.

Jennifer Hockey

Today I Threw Away a Photograph

Today I threw away a photograph I've had with me for some
    time.
Before I turned it out I divided it into four, then eight, then
    more.
I made it into something so small no one would have guessed
    what it had once been.
Only I knew.

I spread the little pieces across my table
and picked through them with a pair of tweezers.
I found an eye, almost intact, and a piece of mouth,
not cheek, because it was fleshy and your cheek was never
    flesh-coloured.
I looked for your hair and found some.
I collected all the little bits together and turned them over.
Underneath, nothing.
Just an off-white blank where I suppose your brain should
    have been.
I scooped all the pieces into my hands
and cradled them there for a minute.
They felt light and helpless, and I shook them about a little.
Then I didn't know where to put you.
What to do with you now?
I took a pair of knickers that were drying across the radiator
and dropped you into them, down into the crutch.
You lay there like little crumbs in the bottom of a hammock.
I swung you gently from side to side.
Then I screwed the knickers into a tight ball and put them on
    to a baking tray.
I baked you at Gas Mark 7 for 45 minutes.
When I took you out
All I found was a sticky mess
clinging to the bottom of my singed knickers.

J. Hollis

72

Ms. Do–As–You–Would–Be–Done–By

Ms. do–as–you–would–be–done–by
wasn't being 'done' half enough
but when she had a go at 'doing'
her husband got in a huff
he said men were the ones to do 'doing'
and women must lay back and be 'done'
so Ms. do–as–you–would–be–done–by
handed him a four-foot marrow
and said
stick
that
up yer bum

Fran Landsman

I Hate Dan

I hate Dan
Him and his boozy clan.
He should be banned
from having a stand
in this 'ere land.
That alki git
wants a bit
of my tit
makes me shit
Hell on earth
He's not worth
the phlegm in my spit
Dan Mills kills
the life in me.

Meena Rane

A Battered Wife

Purple, black – all shades of love
Kicked into a patchwork on my body.
'Sorry' being a much longed for word:
But not to 'half a woman', 'a nobody',
No longer a wife, just a 'thing'.
A nothing, a walking ache.
Love could help, his love –
But not friends, or doctors.
Outsiders being the final mistake.
Hanging together by the fear
Not the ultimate peace of death,
But the fear of being totally unloved,
Not being anwered 'Why?' until
His fingers on my throat stop my breath.
Legs, body, back, head, breasts
Connected to me by strings of pain,
Just a puppet devoid of a soul
Dangling inside a black wedding frame.

Kate Thompson

For Mother
Born 1918 Died 1981

I was four years old
when you married him.
How well
I remember, being confused and horrified
watching my new daddy
beating his fists on the table
screaming at you.
He would browbeat you
until he had utter obedience.
You were carrying his child.
Helplessly I stood,
an onlooker, while he beat you.
Your breasts full of milk
and bruises.
You bore him my sister
which led to a duet of terrified screams,
begging him,
Please, leave our mammy alone.

I was nine years old
when I first took you to hospital.
They treated your jagged nerves,
stitched your gaping wounds.
But your only comfort
was the escapism of alcohol,
And later,
A hospital for alcoholics.
Time and time again
they repaired you
only
to send you back
for him
to brutalise.

Semi-darkened bedroom
a shaft of sunlight slants through closed curtains,
Standing looking down on you.
Mother of mine,
You lay so still
with shaky fingers.
I touch you,
Kiss your cold, stiff face.
My selfish pain begs you,
wake up – hold me.
I am a mother myself.
Now I know you had no choice –
the streets with your two daughters
or
the persecution from a violent, dominant man.
I carry our painful scars.
Goodbye mother,
at last you have found
Your eternal
              refuge . . .

Joy Larraine

The Daisy Field

The telephone breaks through my sleep.
'Is that you darling? Mummy here.'
A girl's voice still
in this her ninetieth year.

Warm grass and cuckoo-sharpened air,
the buttercup glowed gold beneath her chin.
Five-year-old fingers worked
green, yellow, white, encircled hair
and limbs with gentle chains.
Four decades on, they still hang there,
'Is that you, darling? Mummy here.'

Angela Kirby

Soup

From the lighted window
I watch my mother
picking leeks in the twilight.

I will have soup
for my supper,
sprinkled with green parsley.

She passes me my creamy bowl.
My hands are warm,
and smell of soap.

My mother's hands are cold as roots.
She shuts up the chickens
by moonlight.

Selima Hill

For Christianne

I am cutting her peats
Standing for hours in the sleety rain
Plunging the blade in the black mud moor
Down, jerk, up, down, jerk, up,
As once she churned butter on a summer's day.
I see white in the hair of her son's bent head
As his still strong hands lift the cold peat slabs.
Each has a hollow where his thumb has held.
The sky is grey, the gulls fly low.
Her kitchen is smokey, steamy-warm.
She opens the small stove door and thrusts
Another fibrous parcel into the dull red ash.
I like to see her there, moving lightly
From kettle to broth-pot to hot fire flames
Rearranging her patterns of spouts and handles and sticking
    up spoons,
Not shivering through a cold wet morning
Bowed with peat buckets in the wind and rain
While her old man weeps that he is weak and she an aged
    queen.

Susan Maciver

Blinis

Tonight as I prepared them,
Puffed, small and dappled brown
As they should have been,
I thought of Baboushka
In the long Parisian afternoons
Flattening the bubbles of flour
with a worn wooden spoon and stirring,
stirring the honey-coloured cream.
I was allowed to whip the egg whites dry
and paint a swirl of butter in the pan.
I don't remember eating them,
Just the stooped, content old lady
So engrossed and certain of her art.
Later, she would take me through
The spotted, curling photographs
That lined her walls with comfort
And bring me to her other life –
A sepia land of country dachas, carriages
And wooden colonels taking tea.
We journeyed far from the damp, small flat,
With the ikons by the door, on the right,
The dust-woven rugs from Algeria
And the little, blackened blinis pan.

Baboushka, my life is fast and easy now;
I do not use your old and slow techniques,
But should it change as yours did
And leave me unprepared,
Please pray for me,
For I've lost my Bible and my wooden spoon.

Felicity Napier

The Maids

In the kitchen
A parlourmaid sulks in a chair
Stroking the calf of her black-stockinged leg
She's mourning for her sailor
With his blond curly hair
How she longs for his kiss
To be stamped across her throat
For his words to fall deep inside her
As her body starts to float

In the cowshed
A milkmaid lurks in the gloom
She wears a cotton frock
And giggles into her hand
Her cheeks are wet with little specks of rain
She's been driving her cattle home
Down a silver lane

In the cellar
A barmaid hallucinates with the boys
Jumps up on the table
Screaming for more noise
'I just want to feel you.'
She says with a moan,
'I just want to feel you
To make sure I'm not alone.'

In the bedroom
A chambermaid turns down the sheets
Empties the pot
And lays out a wreath

Jehane Markham

Marianne

It took three of them
To hold her down.
She didn't want
To lie there.
Dogs had
Been there.
She didn't want
Any beer.
Her face turned
To the wet grass:
    Brit-lover. Bitch . . .
His mad face.
The bottle.
Spit on his mad face.
The empty bottle.
She knew what the
Game was then:
    Holy Mary, Mother of God . . .

The writhing ground.
The bladed grass.
No one holding her
Any more.

The constable thought
He'd stumbled across
The beast with two backs
After late-night dancing.

The men in the white room
Said they couldn't
Stop the bleeding
So they took it all away.

The virgin womb.
The Judas glass.

Then the priest came
Scurrying with
Saints in his eye.

Pam Bridgeman

Naked Bodies

The cripple boy sat, so that from where I was lying
His knee
seemed to brush
My breast.
I watched him for an hour,
holding a stick of charcoal between
His stumps.
His arms ended at the elbow.
On the left stump was
a horrible
deformed
forked
digit.
With a nail.
His body was squat.
He rolled along with a sea gait,
coming into the studio.
I felt my nakedness keenly.
Right. Wrong. Perfect. Imperfect.
Watched his fleshy stumps
move over the paper
in the diffuse afternoon light,
in the bright studio.
He had a beautiful face, like a young romantic hero.
And his shoulders swooped and curved
gracefully
as he worked.
His desire pricked
My skin
like hot sweat.
Pungent.
Urgent.
I felt his breath on my face,
his skin rubbing, exciting mine.
He took me.
With that charcoal, those stumps,

And his Italian lover's eyes,
He stirred
My flesh.

Caroline Douglas

Colonised

I am afraid of footsteps
they bring anxiety
suspense
a sense of dread and apprehension
mounting step by step
to fear.

With measured steps
he stalks the creaking stairs
heaving his heavy flesh
with rigid rhythm towards me
in my hiding place
my room under the roof
my prison.

My heart is jumping, hurting in my chest.
What will it be this time?
Will he be calling me for supper,
sending me for cigarettes?
Or will it be like last time
when he brought marzipan and raisins and an apple
things I love but hate from him
and then his heavy hand on me, my knee, my thigh.

From fear to terror
as the frightful steps stop outside the door,
a pregnant pause filled with the fear of pain
and then his giant figure in the frame
his grin of shame
his hand held out to offer me a grapefruit
gift of guilt
astringent, bitter.

All this feels wrong to me.
Yes, wrong!
But can it be?
Can he really be so wrong,
my father, my protector?

Has he perhaps a right to me
to do as he likes with his daughter?
If he has not
what am I to think or feel or do?
Dare I protest, should I say no
would he allow me to?
I know he would not.

    O God, please help me:
    Make him go away!
    Just that,
    and I'll never tell,
    never even think of it again:
        (God did not listen to my cry for help to save me from
        this treacherous intrusion nor would he ease the agony of
        my tormented mind or lift the anguish of my deepening
        confusion or heal the hurt in my bewildered heart. No
        one there to shield me from the shock of shame or share
        the awful knowing of never struggling clear of the
        sharpening shadows of despair creeping into my soul,
        settling there, and changing the course of my becoming
        to   not becoming   me.)

Later on the bed where I should lie for comfort
and he for warmth against me, stroking, probing,
I was not comforted nor warmed,
only afraid:

Terror throbbing in my throat
his heavy body rocking hard on mine
his breath, his flesh so hideously near
his eyes not seeing me, my fear
his strange excitement sickening me.

    If I'm sick now
    I know I shall die
    I know he'll kill me
    but if I lie
    completely still

suspended in silent fear
I may survive.

I did survive, many a time, but not intact.
Feelings of unspeakable disgust,
   for him locked into lust
   and for me suffering these sinister proceedings
   silently for years in a paralysis of guilt and shame,
lingered for long like an illness in my heart
unhealed.

The worst of it was that,
going down for supper after the first time,
shaken, soiled, diminished
but hoping still for help from my mother,
I found in shock, that I could not look into her eyes,
simply could not raise my eyes to hers
to tell her of my terror.

Because I lost her then forever
(stopped waiting for her love)
something in me died
while understanding for the first time fully
her reasons for not loving me:
she must have known, all along, right from the beginning
how bad I was!
(Or so I thought)
and I forgave her then
for simply not being able to love me.

Is this another way, they the fathers
split us off one from another,
mother from daugher, daughter from mother?

Frauke Hansen

My Step-daughter

My step-daughter's having
Her father's child.
My child is his child too.
One day
He may want to
Have my child's child.
It's a manly thing to do.

Anonymous

Greenham New Year

Still cold with night and the shedding of an old year,
The trees leant forward and hid us.
The bracken softened into silence
And even the birds held their breath
For longer than the breaking of a normal dawn.
Like ancient people, scaling ancient walls,
We tipped the glinting, clunking aluminium
Upwards, towards the disappearing stars,
And hard against the piercing of the wire.
In the distance, coming quickly
Like the dawn, but laser-fine
And yellow-iced, a new light came.
Turning the wheel, they aimed and fired,
And in the sudden and exploding brightness
We played our scene, like swift
And darting moths in amber.

Leaping and flying,
Brand-new witches, lighter than the wind,
And they, big men in bigger boots,
Sucked at by the cloying clay,
Fat with duty and disadvantaged
By running with their eyes closed,
They had so little chance.
Holding hands and touching,
Laughing as we gasped for breath,
We galloped and sprang
Forty feet to the very top,
And danced
In the dawn upon their grave,
The one they'd made for us.
And there at the tip of the world
We breathed the air of morning,
Gulping in mouthfuls
Of the New Year freshly birthed.
And then we knew it was too late and late enough.

We'd won.
Their obscene mound could never be the same.
We'd put our touch on it,
We had marked it with our violet flowers,
Chanted, sung and danced upon it.
We took strange precautions,
Issued strange proscriptions.
We had joined our hands
In the circle that cannot be broken.

We had moved in unison
Against the clock and towards the sun.
We had made life ring out
Upon their concrete, half-made heap of death.

And when they came, as we all knew they would,
Smart-uniformed, with dog and chain,
(But with a puzzled look),
We simply sat, and in the freezing rain
We laughed as they dragged us all away.
For in the growing light of day, we saw
Their faces, and could tell
That even they had realised
They'd come too late.

Carole Harwood

Romance – 1943

The wind blows over the yellowing grass
Outside in the rain . . .
Silver the arrows of the rain
That pierce the mud of the aerodrome.
The hangars droop, the runways shine,
And the Wellingtons settle deeper into the mud.
Surely the weather is not fit for flying?
Surely I shall see my love tonight?
To be with him once, to talk to him again,
After the empty weeks.

After the waiting the reward is
To be together,
But the talk will be either of flying or beer,
Friendly and masculine.
(Minus his airspeed indicator
Bill did a perfect landing –
A good show that, in filthy weather.)
The young Australian faces with blue eyes
Laugh through the smoke and the drink and the singing
(Going on in the bar-parlour with a tinkly piano).
This is fun! This is life!
Now they're breaking glasses, the party's really going.

Don't spoil it by getting serious.
There's a war on! We're not in love –
How can we be when he gets killed tomorrow?
So don't spoil it, my child, when we say goodbye
By looking up and crying into the huge and trembling trees.
Here he is, so near and real,
Human and happy and a little bit tight.
If he wants to make love to me I'll let him,
But it's not serious, not tender and lovely and heartbreaking.

Romance is gone with Keats' nightingale –
This is today.
The bombers roar in over the hedges

Coming in to land.
Goodnight quickly, my love, I love you,
But where my heart was there is now a stone,
For you will be dead tomorrow,
Your youth twisted in the wreckage of a machine . . .
And I will not, I must not cry.

We are a strong generation and we shall know
This to be over in due time,
And the reward of our agony will arise
From ashes of this dusty, ruined earth –
Avenues and gardens and palaces –
And bells and thunderous symphonies
To fill the liberated skies.

M.P.S. Denton

Strangers

Tonight after a long, long bath
I wrapped him in a warm soft towel
and carried him upstairs, like a baby.

He held on to me
gap-toothed and smiling
I placed him gently on the bed
then brought him bread and honey and apple
and we read of a boy who went to sea.

He slept.

Today he called me a 'fucker' (six times)
told me to 'shut up'
screamed, tore my calendar,
scattered his clothes over the floor
tried to lock himself in with a ten-inch bike lock
shouted 'Why? Why? Why?'
and spent his pocket-money on a bag of soldiers and tanks
then sat out in the spring sunshine
playing war.

Kath McKay

She Could Do With A Backfire Bomber

She could do with a backfire bomber
wind
        unbinds
                the lady on the bike
upskirts her

                with a squirt
it flips the lid
                off little silo
as he idles
            in the street

                        whips out
the private parts
                of thoughts

a flying button

and a real
cruise missile
            of a whistle

                                Gillian Allnutt

Whatweakersex?

There's one thing I've always wanted to do
cos I think it'd be such fun.
It's to go round pinching every man I see
firmly on the bum.
To watch them blush and edge away
would be my greatest thrill.
On tubes and crowded pavements
I'd be out to kill.
I'd pull a hefty handful of flesh
from off their manly cheek,
or perhaps I'd try a simpler style
and perfect a gentle tweak.
Denim bums and pinstripe bums
I'd give them all fair share,
a pinch just hard enough to prove
that tweaker sex was there.

Fran Landsman

I Had Rather Be A Woman

I had rather be a woman
Than an earwig
But there's not much in it sometimes.
We both crawl out of bed
But there the likeness ends.
Earwigs don't have to
Feed their children,
Feed the cat,
Feed the rabbits,
Feed the dishwasher.
They don't need
Clean sheets,
Clean clothes,
Clean carpets,
A clean bill of health.
They just rummage about
In chrysanthemums.
No one expects them
To have their
Teetotal, vegetarian
Mothers-in-law
To stay for Christmas,
Or to feel a secret thrill
At the thought of extending the kitchen.
Earwigs can snap their pincers at life
And scurry about being quite irresponsible.
They enjoy an undeserved reputation
Which frightens the boldest child.
Next time I feel hysterical
I'll bite a hole in a dahlia.

Daphne Schiller

The Prince

Ok Prince! with a kiss
You have awoken me to bliss
It is incumbent upon me to be happy ever after
And indulge in mirth and laughter
I suppose. And yet, and yet.
I touched a prick, the resultant fears
Kept me sound asleep for a hundred years:
So what have you to offer?

Audrey Insch

Tea Break 11.05

From just looking,
Reflecting
Idly,
I'd bet you make love
Like you swim breaststroke –
    Chin forward
    Neck bull-thick
    Body powerful
    Bobbing and bowing
    To the surge of your
    Shoulders and legs.
Me drinking coffee
As you sit there
With your heavy, casual arm
Fitting the round back of the girl
Who mirrors your mother
In portable silence.

Louise Heal

Blue Moves

Slippy slippy fingers
Prowling in the crack.
Foregone resignation
Rolls round on its back.
Mounting isolation
Drives the message home,
In sex and drugs and rock and roll
We both have come
Undone.

Jennifer Hockey

Dirty Work

They have been here before us
those other ones
leaving the air disturbed
a bloom of finger-
marks on the furniture
burns on the fumed oak.

Did they put their cases
side by side
on the thin carpet,
lock the door,
tell bad jokes,
blow dust and hair
from the bedside tables, think
the stain on the ceiling
looks like Australia?

You unwrap champagne
I open caviare
we share one spoon,
it takes more
than a hard bed
and a sixty-watt bulb
to put us off.
But the bottle
looks out of place
here, embarrassed,
like gentry
at a village wedding.

When the last bubble
bursts we stand
hand in hand at the window.
Look, you say,
even the glass is dirty.
You breathe on it,
trace arrows, hearts

initials, love–
in–a–mist while I
wonder if those other
lovers stood like this,
flicked at the peeling paint
and imagined the street lights
were brighter than usual.

Angela Kirby

Brief Encounter

Rain, Saturday afternoon,
the two of us watching
the exquisite tragic face
of a youthful Celia Johnson,
as I do the ironing.
I have stood on all those platforms,
sat on hard high stools in station bars,
sipped tea from coarse-rimmed cups
and specks of dust have blurred my gaze.
I recognise the silences,
the ease of her small deceptions.

Nothing tragic or exquisite
here, at home –
just the hiss of my iron
on clean, legitimate shirts
but beyond them other men's clothes
and rumpled sheets and hair,
relentless clocks, at stations
and bedsides, ticking away
in the darkness, disapproving . . .
the wall between us more unscalable
with each brief encounter.

'Thank you for coming home,'
her husband says,
irony glinting in their cosy grate.
I look across at you on the sofa,
then down at your Monday shirt
and hear the sound of departing trains
as I fix the little buttons.
I fold it carefully,
recreate you in its flatness,
then bend as if to kiss the sweet clean smell
knowing this is all there is.

Felicity Napier

Anger

The day you said you loved her and not me
I just saw red.

I saw your rude, sexy, red tongue part my seventeen–year–old
    lips,
And I wanted white–hot, searing metal to brand FOREVER
    on your mouth.

I saw you eagerly slip your gold band past my red, manicured
    nail,
And I wanted to gouge out your eye from your mind's
    seething offal.

I saw our red–letter day when you got your promotion,
And I wanted to screw the champagne bottle into your balls.

I saw our slippery, sweet, newborn, red son; and your pride,
    your joy and your tears,
And I knew I would tell him that you didn't love him.

I saw a long, fiery–red scratch down the small of your back
– that wasn't like me!

And I wanted the courage to face up to truth and/or change,
Preferring instead to unplug my mind and store it away in
    A dark, dusty cupboard.

I saw a brand–new red sports car call to take you away,
And I wanted youth and beauty and money and flair and
    charm
and poise and elegance and wit and intellect and you.

But you'd gone.

I saw raw, hacked, red wrists, red veins spewing red blood,
Because my anger wanted a victim.

Helen Roberts

Snake In The Grass

Now that you've sloughed me off
so neatly,
flickering out of my life
in your smooth new skin,
eyes bright and forked tongue
a little moist in anticipation,
do not look back.

I am still here in the dark,
hidden by last year's leaves,
brittle, paper-thin and empty.
A few scales are missing
but I hold your shape for ever.

Angela Kirby

In the Railway Station

There are mad old women
who carry all their property
in a little bundle on their backs.

Vagrants who curl up
at night in the railway station.
People dying in hospital
waiting for what will be
their last operation.

And I have wasted so much time
with you.

Anna 'Swir'

Wives

Katherine of Aragon,
traded and shipped,
passed from brother to brother
to combine with royal potency.

How many times was it
you failed to deliver;
pushed out the rocks
that would batter?
A girl, a runt, to quick death.
The great bed was a desert.

Did your esoteric rosaries
anger the moon,
a midwife,
a dark angel?

Dying alone, you write:
'The tender love I owe you
forceth me (my case being such)
to commend myself to you . . .
mine eyes desire you
above all things,'
and asked a marriage portion
for each of your maids.

They mourned
with a pavane and a masque,
whilst, like a sword from Calais
for a stone lozenge,
the new queen sharpened her tongue.

But daily
the bond grew stronger:
keepers of poor eggs
chewing on herbs,
panicking deep in the month
for cradles, cradles.

Cradles, cradles.
Little white plums between the legs.
For the boy-child, the prize is burial
with the lavish and ulcerous king.

Verity Carter

Napisanity

I soaked the nappies in a bucket
kneaded them like dough
pinned them to the line,
flags of surrender,
proud of their whiteness.

I folded them in lines,
in drawers.
Like shrouds
they lay in darkness
until one by one
they dressed her soft peach flesh
and
stained.

I soaked the nappies in a bucket,
kneaded them like dough,
pinned them to the line,
flags of surrender,
water running from their edges like grief.

Christine Aziz

Our Connection Was Severed

Our acquaintance
was dodgy from the start;
in the very first week
I was sick as a dog for you,
grumping away in my stomach –
what a liberty!

By the third month
the strain began to tell;
like an alien invader
you drained my resources,
my inadequate resources.
By the fourth month
the strain began to kill.
The doctor said
'You will have a miscarriage –
or you may die first.
Do you agree, Mrs Pemberthy? Do you agree
we should terminate the pregnancy now?'
I said 'Terminate . . .
Terminate . . .'
so she–he–it was terminated.
Our connection was severed.

You came at the wrong time
to the wrong person.
It wasn't my fault
that you were misdirected.
I posted you 'Return to Sender' –
may the universal powers
take you to their hearts.

And for a while
you were part of me . . .
Sometimes I see
a small, squashed face
pressed against the glass

of the lighted shop–window of life.
Then the bitter tears stream down
like broken waters.
The waters break, bitter and resurgent . . .
Had you lived
you would have wept harder, wept longer.
My eyes shed your tears,
My body bears your pain.

It is all I can do.

Fay Chivers

Blood

When the moon swings round
And I bleed my woman's blood
My belly swells and sings to me
a low knowing chant.
Then something dark, akin to witches,
Heaves and turns, and I feel a strength
An invincible power.
I dream a foetus blooming on high blood tides,
Possibility kicking my guts,
A baby shaped like shackles and chains
Smiles sickly and selfish eyes.
How sweet you moon–devil child,
Waiting for my pale soul–sister to make you flesh.
Leech! You would suck my self to dust.
I was not born for this!
Though moon and blood conspire against
my flat belly,
I will deny this blatant fertility.

Caroline Douglas

Waste

Long white hairs, thick, wavy, that twine
into sweaters, carpets, wrap themselves
round the head of the vac. as it whines
over bedroom floors, under kitchen shelves.
Bullet tampons in shiny cellophane
that swell, soften, absorb blood and mucous,
are dropped on a string to linger in blocked drains.
I push my wrist up the U-bend, provoke a gush
of bloody cotton wool, cardboard, shit,
pour soda crystals, boiling water into
the smeary bowl, wait for their caustic grit
to work, wash my hand and arm to the elbow,
pump the chromium handle until there is no smell
only water sucking at porcelain flesh.

Patricia Pogson

114

Family Planning

my mum said that babies
always come from storks
my friend says they're from something
which sounds a bit like 'forks'
i think she's wrong though
but i do know what stops them altogether
it's . . . er . . . um . . . er . . . oh yeh . . . corks

Fran Landsman

Latch-Key Kid

'But what will you do in the holidays?' the interviewer said.
What indeed?
What was there to do with my sweet-natured, latch-key kid
but deny her existence,
or rent or invent a granny or mother-in-law
or give up the idea of working at all?
'My first husband takes her to stay,' I lied,
as though the country was crowded with cast-off husbands of
    mine,
'we're on excellent terms.'
I smooth down the folds of my pinafore dress
and blink at my brand-new past.
The man rumbles on, like far-away thunder,
'and after school, half-term, what happens then?'

Ah, what happens then?

I flick through the years,
playgroups and nurseries, child-minders, neighbours and
    friends,
the impossible places reached on lumbering always-late
    buses,
the hours that never quite matched with the hours at work,
the guilt,
the hum of exhaustion like telephone wires in the wind.

'My sister,' I said, 'she takes her.'
'She lives down the road,
and my aunt on occasion, nextdoor but one,
but anyway, Gran's in the attic,
I've an out-of-work nursery teacher renting the downstairs
    flat
and two substitute mothers on permanent call.'

Well, what could he say?
That I lied?
That he didn't like communal living?

That I had too many family ties?
That he wanted somebody younger, more mobile?

Well, he did.

What *was* there to do with my sweet-natured, latch-key kid
but deny her existence?

Penny Windsor

Love The Children

Love the children
better than light
or the powers
of marriage.

The children
see through darkness
and the secrets of silence,
they are more than alive
even when they sleep.

Their perfect guesses
protect us from what we know best.
Their courage
floats on wings
like a summer
we must avoid
for it is too vivid for us.
We remain
on our narrow, cold fjords,
ice chaining our feet.

Penelope Shuttle

Classroom Politics

They will not forgive us
These girls
Sitting in serried rows
Hungry for attention
Like shelves of unread books,
If we do not
Make the world new for them,
Teach them to walk
Into the possibilities
Of their own becoming,
Confident in their exploring.

They will not forget
If we do not use
Our often-surrendered positions
On the front line
To wage war against
The subtle hordes of male historians
Who constantly edit female experience
And endlessly anthologise
Their own achievements.

They will not accept
The old excuses of their foremothers
If they grow up to find
That we have betrayed them.

Fiona Norris

The Cow Loves Her

Her children
have long since ceased to write to her.
Now
only the cow loves her.

It's only natural,
after all, she's cared for it
since it was born.

Anna 'Swir'

Dulcie Celebrates at The Old White Horse, Brixton

Brandy and Babycham at the double!
I've said goodbye to all me troubles.
He's taken his clothes and the benefit book.
He slammed out the door so the whole place shook.
For the good of me health I'd got under the bed
So me poor rotten furniture copped it instead.

Port and lemon and make it snappy!
Tomorrow I'll know how it feels to be happy.
I'll save me money and clear off the debts.
I'll clean the place of him and have no regrets
Make an appointment to sort out me veins
And learn to enjoy meself over again.

God knows what state my mascara's in.
He needn't think I was weeping for him.
I hadn't expected to burst into tears
Till I thought of his fist and the six months' arrears.

Rum and blackcurrant before they call time
From now on I'll know just what's what and what's mine.
I'll get on a diet and get on the Pill
There's a few good years left to me still.
A bit of peace and a bit of fun
And a moment or two to meself in the sun.

God knows where he's gone to. I hope he's alright
Cos if he can't turn up a bed for the night
If he's hungry and lonely, then knowing my Jack,
He'll be bloody angry, he'll be bloody back.

Beverley Ireland

Aunt Bet

It's morning, and she shuffles through
in pink quilted
nylon gown and I'm still cramped,
shut on the put–you–up.
    'Hello darling, you awake? I'll bring
    you tea.'
I snap out and dress fast, she
pees loudly, puts in toast and I
clear last night's cigarettes off the
coffee table
    'What time are you out, darling
. . . I'm going to the . . . em . . .
the physio . . .
ten o'clock darling,
we can leave together then,
lovely!'

The automatic toast jumps up
and lands down the back of the spin–drier.
We drink tea by the oven while
pulling out butter and plates
to have breakfast by the fire,
three spoonfuls of cornflakes for my Aunt Bet.

At half–past nine she begins to shed her nightclothes
to dress for today.
Old lady, baby–bare,
woman as I,
from her gaunt shoulder–blades
to her rolling belly.

I lay her purple spotted nighty across the armchair
and she steps into a Marks
and Spencer's elastic suit with dangling clips.
    'All–in–ones have always been best for me'
pokes in her soft wrinkly breasts,
shoulder–straps next,

she lifts her right arm like an oar,
skirt and jumper 'I do love my woollies!' –
and finally, stockings,
which she sits down to do herself.

    'Last week I was hopeless,
just hopeless, with these suspender buttons . . .'
She jokes and finds her shoes.
      'I feel I'm on the way up now.
I'm beginning to get things
as they used to be . . .
but I don't worry about time now . . .
I used to be dreadful!
dreadful!
everything had to be done that day
just right, and if I didn't . . .
but now I just don't bother.'

We leave together and kiss goodbye till Wednesday,
and I hope,
hope against hope,
that the loops won't slip before then.

Ruth Marshall

The Appointment

She stared at the blue between the strips of blinds
while the good-looking, grey-haired surgeon
washed and washed his hands. He kept her talking
so that when he turned he could look at her eyes
and not at her bare and nervous breasts.
'I love gardening,' he said, 'I've cut my grass
already.' She wished she could smell it –
new mown – in the room. She climbed on the bed
and her shoes made marks on the paper sheet.
His fingers probed her flesh with expertise
and she thought about her armpits growing moist.
'Sit up now, please.' Hands stole upon her
from behind and all she wanted was to close
her eyes and lean back slowly in his arms.

A button flew off her blouse and both of them
dived to pick it up. She smiled at his offer
of surgical thread. 'We don't need to see you again,'
he said, putting down the file and offering his hand.
She shifted the button from her palm to meet
the fingers that had touched her, then out
she lurched, longing for the streeet, for air,
for the litter and clutter of ordinary people
going about their lives. She must have pushed
the wrong swing-doors. On either side of her
exhausted faces stared from pillows, high and white,
like clouds. She fixed her eyes on the neon EXIT
sign at the end of the long grey corridor, not daring
to look down at the tightrope she was walking on.

Felicity Napier

Sisters

Each new day yawns like an empty chasm
for the near-blind old woman
sitting in her little terraced house.

Ill-defined shapes people her world
dimly lit by the twice-weekly visit
of the paid home-help.

Some neighbours drop in to drink tea
and chat. Others do the shopping.
One, no longer welcome, looked round
at the cluttered chaos and said
    'Couldn't live in a pig-stye.'

Her sister, Joan, eighty, but hale and hearty,
scolds her as she stumbles clumsily
round her shrunken room and says,
    'I don't know why you don't get dressed up
and go out. Look at me, I make the effort.'

One day, flustered by her sister's presence,
she blundered into a chair and fell down.
Joan made no move to help her to her feet
but said, 'By the way, we'd better discuss
it now. Do you want to be buried or cremated?'

Hilda Cohen

On the Way to the Station

Leaves reach out by the thousand to me,
the air is electric with sunlight.
'Listen, *Listen*!' they say,
'Let us come with you,
walk beside you, stroke your hair,
hover round like crowds of children,
like clouds of loving rain.'
'I can't,' I say,
'I'm going to town.
My sister needs me to collect her mail
talk to the banker
see to the dog.'
I turn away.
My hair is combed.
I've gotten my ticket,
and so the greenery turns pale
in the dust of the train window.

Her house isn't far from the station.
I go to the garden in back,
but bindweed now covers the gate,
the path,
and most of the lawn, and there –
new grass has sprouted on
what must be the
grave of her collie.
A peephole rubbed weakly through the grime of the window.
I call her solicitor
who takes care of everything,
says goodbye quickly
while scribbling some notes.
On the way back
a café looks tidy
but I can't go in.
I have to get home
see to the canary

check the mail
and comb my greying hair.

Her Belly

She has a right to have a fat belly,
her belly has borne five children.
They warmed themselves at it,
it was the sun of their childhood.

The five children have gone,
her fat belly remains.
This belly
is beautiful.

Anna 'Swir'

Two Old Women

The two of us sit in the doorway
chatting about our children and grandchildren.
We sink happily
into our oldwomanhood.

Like two spoons
sinking
into a bowl of hot porridge.

Anna 'Swir'

Immortal

She moved out of herself
a long time ago.

With each new grandchild
she begins life anew
like a river renewed each moment
from its source.

Gazing always at the sky
with the eyes of the newborn
she won't notice
the death of her body.

Anna 'Swir'